Objects and Stories

Links to the Past 1

Pearson Australia
(a division of Pearson Australia Group Pty Ltd)
707 Collins Street, Melbourne, Victoria 3008
PO Box 23360, Melbourne, Victoria 8012
www.pearson.com.au

First published 2012 by Pearson Australia
2016 2015 2014 2013
10 9 8 7 6 5 4 3 2

Author: Liz Flaherty
Publisher: Sarah Russell
Project Editor: Rachel Davis
Editor: Sally Bullen
Designers: Anne Donald and Cameron McPhail
Copyright & Pictures Editor: Alice McBroom
Desktop Operator: Kate Hansen
Cover Designer: Glen McClay
Printed in Australia by the SOS Print + Media Group

National Library of Australia Cataloguing-in-Publication entry
Author: Flaherty, Liz, 1963-
Title: Links to the past 1 / Liz Flaherty.
ISBN: 9781442559776 (pbk.)
Series: Objects and stories.
Notes: Includes index.
Target Audience: For primary school age.
Subjects: History--Juvenile literature.
Material culture--Juvenile literature.
Dewey Number: 909

Pearson Australia Group Pty Ltd ABN 40 004 245 943

Acknowledgements
We would like to thank the following for permission to reproduce copyright material.
Mitchell, John: pp. 21, 23.
Pearson Australia: Alice McBroom, pp. 5, 7, 8, 9, 11, 13, 14, 15, 17, 19, 20, 25, 26, 27, 29.
Shutterstock: cover.

Every effort has been made to trace and acknowledge copyright. However, if any infringement has occurred, the publishers tender their apologies and invite the copyright holders to contact them.

Disclaimers
The selection of internet addresses (URLs) provided for this book was valid at the time of publication and was chosen as being appropriate for use as a primary education research tool. However, due to the dynamic nature of the internet, some addresses may have changed, may have ceased to exist since publication, or may inadvertently link to sites with content that could be considered offensive or inappropriate. While the authors and publisher regret any inconvenience this may cause readers, no responsibility for any such changes or unforeseeable errors can be accepted by either the authors or the publisher.

Some of the images used in *Objects and Stories: Links to the Past 1* might have associations with deceased Indigenous Australians. Please be aware that these images might cause sadness or distress in Aboriginal or Torres Strait Islander communities.

Thank you to everyone who generously shared their story from the past.

Contents

Words that are printed in bold are explained in the Glossary on page 31.

Introduction

Most people have a story or something special in their lives that links them to their past.

Our stories are important. They are part of who we are and where we come from. Sharing stories keeps us connected to our past. In this book, you will meet some people who will share their story about the past with you.

Stories can be told in different ways. Some stories are shared through **oral** storytelling, shared between family members and passed down from one **generation** to the next. Other stories are told through important objects, such as photos, letters, jewellery or even a car! Some of the people in this book have a special object that links them to their past.

Emma's nanna has passed on her Polish **heritage** to Emma and her daughters.

Meet Thanh

Thanh is a talented artist. She uses her artwork to tell important stories.

Thanh uses different **mediums** in her artwork. The different types of paint and materials she uses help her to express feelings and tell stories in lots of ways. Thanh's sculpture called "The **Migrants**" tells a special story about her experience of being a **refugee**.

Thanh and her family of seven left Vietnam in 1979 to **migrate** to Australia. They travelled by boat to Malaysia and came to Australia in 1980.

This is Thanh and her sculpture, "The Migrants", which shares her story of being a refugee.

Thanh's sculpture reminds her of her past and the dangerous journey her family made to Australia. Her sculpture expresses her feelings about **refugees** and their desire for a safe life. It tells a story about people who are heading into an unknown future.

Meet Kevin

Kevin has loved the Beatles for almost 50 years. In the 1960s, the Beatles were the most famous band in the world.

Kevin was 13 years old when the Beatles came to Australia in 1964. He was lucky enough to go to one of their concerts.

Kevin still remembers the Beatles concert – it changed his life. Kevin then knew that music was his thing. He bought his first guitar, and it was the start of a lifelong passion.

Kevin loves guitars so much that he has made some of his own. He plays his guitars every day and writes his own songs. He still loves the Beatles and remembers how they first inspired him. Kevin has passed his passion for guitars and music down to his son, Mark.

Kevin's guitars play different types of music.

Meet Brad

Brad has a passion for collecting memorabilia from the 1950s and 1960s. His passion came from his dad, Dean, who collected things from the same era.

As a child, Brad was surrounded by his dad's collection of music, cars and memorabilia from the 1950s and 1960s. Brad spent a lot of time with his dad and his dad's friends, who were also keen collectors. His dad's favourite room was the one where he kept his memorabilia. Brad loved spending time in this room, listening to music and conversations about the latest additions to the collection.

Brad's collection includes his car, which is also from the 1960s.

VIC
HVX-781

Brad's **memorabilia** reminds him of the great times he shared with his dad. Like his dad, he believes that things from the 1950s and 1960s are **unique** because of their bright colours and beautiful designs. Brad's collection links him to his dad.

Meet Matt

Matt's car is unique. It has a long and interesting history. In its former life, it was a hearse.

Matt's car used to belong to a funeral director in Las Vegas in the United States of America. Because Las Vegas is in the desert, the car was painted white so it wouldn't absorb heat from the sun.

Matt's car is called Miss Lily. Matt loves Miss Lily, even though some of his friends won't get into her. They think it's a bit odd driving around in a **hearse**! Matt doesn't mind being in a hearse at all. He thinks Miss Lily is beautiful and loves driving around in her. She gets a lot of attention wherever she goes!

Miss Lily reminds Matt of Las Vegas and times gone by.

YNQ 511
VICTORIA - THE PLACE TO BE.

Meet Eleanor and Olivia

Eleanor and Olivia's great-grandmother, Peggy, collected dolls from countries all over the world.

Peggy's dolls are souvenirs from each country she went to. She collected them to remind her of her trips. The first thing Peggy did when she arrived in a new country was to look for a doll. All of her dolls are dressed in the traditional costume of the country they come from. The Japanese dolls wear kimonos, and the Scottish dolls have bagpipes.

Eleanor and Olivia love their great-grandmother's dolls.

Eleanor and Olivia love the dolls as much as their great-grandmother did. The dolls are a link to their great-grandmother, as well as to the different places she went to during her travels in the 1960s and 1970s.

Meet John

John Mitchell is the mayor of the City of Greater Geelong, the second largest city in Victoria.

John was born in Geelong and has always been interested in his community. Now that he is mayor, he looks after Geelong's **residents** and provides leadership and guidance. He helps make decisions that affect the community.

In many local councils, **mayors** wear special robes and chains on formal occasions. Geelong's **mayoral** chain is made of 18 carat gold. It was made in the late 19th century.

John wears the mayoral chain proudly on formal occasions. There used to be a tradition of adding a link to represent each mayor. However, this ended in 1934 because the chain was becoming too heavy to wear! The mayoral chain links John to all of Geelong's previous mayors.

As John wears the chain, he thinks of all of Geelong's previous mayors.

Meet Kerry

Kerry uses her art to tell stories. Aboriginal people have been sharing their stories orally and through paintings for thousands of years.

Kerry paints in the traditional **Koori** style of the Wathaurong people in Victoria. She paints stories from her past using symbols that her **ancestors** have passed down from one **generation** to the next. Kerry feels a special connection to the Earth and water, and she often includes them in her paintings.

Kerry's art is influenced by her life and her upbringing.

Kerry wants to share her art and her Aboriginal **heritage** with people. She wants people to understand how Aboriginal people live in an **urban** environment today.

Meet Emma

Emma has close links to her Polish grandmother, whose name was Inka. Inka came to Australia in 1947, after World War II.

Inka's family was Jewish. Most of her family did not survive the war. Inka **migrated** to Australia with her only surviving family – her husband and her young daughter, Kris. Kris is Emma's mother.

Emma's nanna loved her new country, but she also loved Poland. Inka shared stories of Poland with Emma. She taught Emma how to make a Polish chocolate cake called babka.

Emma shares the tradition with her children, and they eat babka for every celebration. Emma's nanna also taught her a Polish song called "Sto Lat". Emma's family sings this song at birthday parties. All Inka's grandchildren have learnt to speak some Polish words.

Emma's daughters, Lizzie and Laura, love wearing their Polish costumes that Nanna gave them.

Timeline

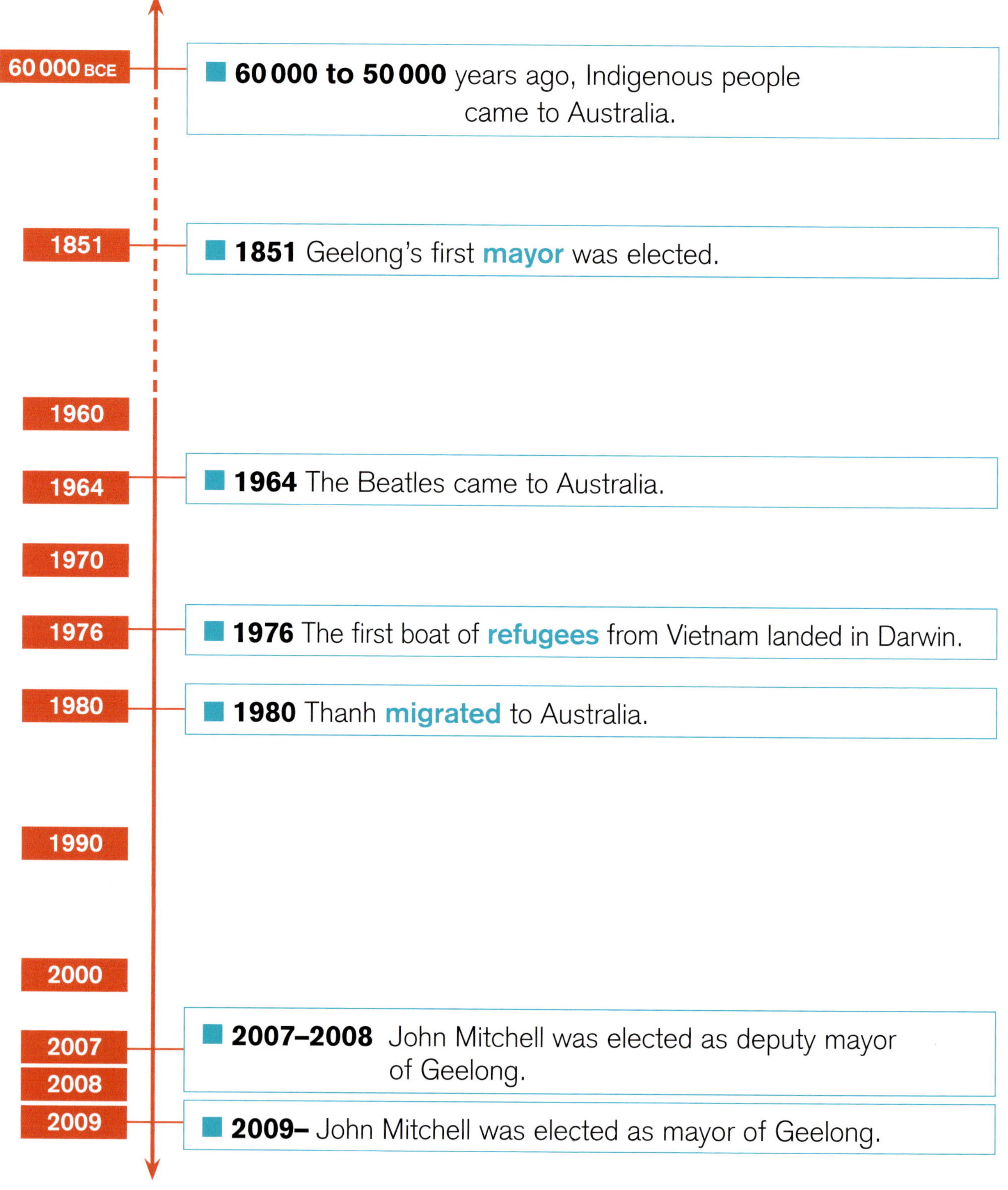

60 000 BCE
■ **60 000 to 50 000** years ago, Indigenous people came to Australia.
1851
■ **1851** Geelong's first **mayor** was elected.
1960
1964
■ **1964** The Beatles came to Australia.
1970
1976
■ **1976** The first boat of **refugees** from Vietnam landed in Darwin.
1980
■ **1980** Thanh **migrated** to Australia.
1990
2000
2007
2008
■ **2007–2008** John Mitchell was elected as deputy mayor of Geelong.
2009
■ **2009–** John Mitchell was elected as mayor of Geelong.

Glossary

ancestors relatives from whom people are descended

era a period of time

generation each stage in a family, such as children, parents, grandparents

hearse a vehicle that carries a coffin to the funeral and cemetery

heritage things that have been passed down through the generations

Koori an Aboriginal person, especially from south-east Australia

mayor the person elected to be the head of a local council of a city or town

mayoral to do with a mayor

mediums different art materials, such as paints, pastels and ink

memorabilia special items from the past that are worth keeping

migrants people who have moved from one place or country to live in another

migrate to move from one place or country to live in another

oral spoken rather than written

orally of spoken language

refugee a person who has left their homeland for safety

residents people who live in a place

unique one of a kind

urban of a town or city

Index